Lauren!
thank you so much for the love & support, girl! I really hope you enjoy this read!

love always,
Emma

KICK THE BOX

PICKING PURPOSE OVER POPULARITY

To my Grandparents – I love you. I miss you. And every day,

I hope you're still proud of me.

-E

TABLE OF CONTENTS

PROLOGUE

Today, Social media is at its peak of popularity. It offers entertainment, means of communication, and also sells identities to those who don't have their own. If you let it, the outside world will pitch you an image of who you should want to be and it'll tell you what you should want to accomplish. By society's standards, we should all be the exact same with no individuality about us at all. The most sought after ambitions we see are money and power. The very last thing this generation promotes is individuality - but it's what we need the most. We'll never lead genuinely happy lives - no matter how successful or powerful - unless we live in a way that is true to who we are and what we stand for. Instead of letting the world dictate and determine what dreams to chase, we must let our hearts spill into our thoughts and actions and move in the direction that was uniquely designed for us and no one else. Achieving this will certainly take more than "thinking outside of the box"! We're going to have to kick that box so far away from us that we can't see it any longer. This box that I speak of represents anything from personal fears to societal pressures.

Instead of focusing on making money, economic status, and the diluted definition of "success", *Kick the Box: Picking Purpose Over Popularity* solely focuses on how to become strong enough mentally to pursue whatever it is that your heart desires. There are several self-help books about dream chasing written by individuals that have "been there, done that", but are now ahead of you and I as far as personal goals. Instead of walking ahead of you and looking back, I'm walking side-by-side with you. I'm still at my starting line like most of you are. As I struggle, you're struggling. As I'm encouraged, you'll be encouraged. You will relate to me, and I to you, on a level that will show you how to push forward in a self-defining way while also reassuring you that

you are not alone on this quest to pursue
what your heart knows is best for you!

YOUR DREAM BELONGS TO YOU

Because there is so much that goes into pursuing your dream, it's crucial that at the end of every long and stressful day you genuinely feel like the effort is worth it solely because you're working towards a goal that you set for yourself to accomplish rather than what someone else wants for you.

The amount of time, effort, and dedication that is required of you during this time of your life will only be meaningful to you if your heart is truly in it for the right reasons. Often times we become unsure of ourselves and the direction in which we're headed so we seek validation outside of our own instinct from people around us.

Wanting to make your loved ones proud is a great thing; as it's always a good thing to have someone that believes in you. However, friends and family members can sometimes persuade us to do and be things that we don't really agree with - but because we love them and value their opinions, we consider their suggestions for our lives and sometimes we run with it as if we came up with it ourselves!

I want you to know that there is a difference between being supported and being pressured by your loved ones. Often times this pressure comes off as "love", but real love would look something like your loved one being supportive and happy for you regardless of what you choose to do with your life. As long as you're happy, they're happy.

It takes courage to boldly pursue what your heart desires to pursue. We're coming of age in a culture that makes it difficult to be confidently authentic.

One minute we're certain that we know what we want to do or who we want to be and we have what it takes to get there, and soon something or someone surfaces and tells us it's "more popular" or "more beneficial" to be someone else or do something else. With this being a constant occurrence – now that social media is as influential as it is - we have to grab ahold of ourselves and refuse to be molded into anything other than who we were created to be! So how do you go about gaining all of this courage to pursue what you really want in spite of what others want for you?

Firstly, you have to acquire and embrace individuality within yourself. You have to be confident in your distinctive identity in order to successfully pursue your dream. I say this because so many people will doubt you throughout your journey that if you don't embody confidence, you'll begin to doubt yourself.

Overtime, social Media has transcended its designed purpose of networking. More recently, it has been given the power to teach the curious, misguide the lost, and corrupt the gullible. Those of us that are hooked on our social network accounts lose a little more individuality every day and are less in-touch with our own reality apart from our cell phones. This is not to imply that having these popular accounts online makes you just like everyone else in a negative way- it's how you allow social media to dictate your life that determines your individuality.

This era is full of trends! There is constantly something to get hip to. Whether it's a new song, fashion statement or aspiration, there always seems to be something that everyone around you adopts at the same time simply because it's what is most popular at that moment. And it's on these social networks that you're introduced to such trends.

While there is nothing wrong with keeping up with current events, it's important to make sure you don't allow society to reshape your purpose. Just like your friends and family shouldn't be able to mold your dream for you, neither should society.

Grab ahold of your purpose and protect it from those who want so badly to change it. You never want to find yourself in a place where you're more loyal to others than you are to your own self. Often times we're more concerned with meeting other people's expectations of us than we are with meeting our own personal expectations. This journey is about you first and foremost. It's everyone else's job to follow your lead - not the other way around.

There are people that will try to convince you to do or be certain things that better fit *their* requirements. However, there are also people that will try to convince you *not* to do or be certain things, as it better fits their *restrictions*. Three common barriers that are bound in place for the purpose of preventing any type of prosperity within a group of people are *racism, sexism, and classism.*

Many job opportunities have been taken away from individuals simply because of the color of their skin or the origin of their descendants. I cannot even count all of the job fields that seem to have an overwhelming amount of one gender working within it over the other – and both women and men deal with this unbalance depending on what career they're pursuing.

Sometimes the reason for such disproportion is because of the conventional history attached to the profession that consists of either a woman or a man "better" fitting the job description contrary to the necessity of equality.

Other times it's the employer's personal prejudice that aims to prevent either gender from advancing in that field. Experiencing the barrier of classism is a little less "in your face", but the impact and purpose of prevention is the same.

People who come from lower class families are often labeled as inferior or less capable. These stigmas hang over our heads every day and as unfortunate as it is, we don't have control over which light people see us under. What we can control is how high we rise above those stigmas no matter who disapproves.

Indefensible efforts such as the restrictions I mentioned are the kinds that have the power to discourage and potentially defeat you *if you allow them to*. Hopefully you're beginning to see why self-awareness and high self-esteem is so important in the early stages of dream chasing. Because when the reality hits that not everybody likes you, believes in you, or even acknowledges you, being in tune with who you are and why you're here is what will save you and push you along.

If no one else thinks so, *you* have to believe you're competent. If no one else says so, *you* have to declare that what you see in your future will come to pass.

So many people envision their dream as a fictitious idea. Whether it is a dream car, dream job, or generally what you see your entire life being like "ideally". We sit in our homes or at our jobs and wonder how great it would be to have this or do that, and after about thirty seconds of daydreaming, it's back to reality. But who said our dreams can't be our reality?

We live in a world where image means everything. Everywhere you turn you see fame and fortune. There are celebrities and public figures that are idolized by millions of people and are put into a category that only certain people belong in - according to society. There's "them" and then there are regular people like you and me. We see the magazines and the reality TV shows as we subconsciously make these people out to be a different species than us.

You tell yourself that you'll never be like them or live their life. And guess what? You're absolutely right! You'll never be like them because you're uniquely you! And you'll never live their life because you have been given your very own life to live with an entirely different story that will birth your very own accomplishments.

The word "success" has been exploited so badly that very few people know how to define it anymore. You don't need to be famous or rolling around in millions of dollars in order to feel successful. Success is the accomplishment of an aim or purpose - plain and simple. If you set out to accomplish something - no matter how minor or major it may be - and you accomplish that goal, you're indeed successful. Having this knowledge is essential because whenever you have a moment of doubt or discouragement, you have to be able to genuinely be content with your decisions and accomplishments or else you'll be distracted by how everyone else's life appears to be compared to yours.

One of the worst things that you could do to yourself is live in competition with others and live for other people. You can only work your hardest for something that you want for yourself. No matter how good someone else's idea is, it won't hold the same significance as an idea of your own.

We live in an influential day in age and Pop Culture will alter your thoughts, actions, and desires if you let it. Someone may have convinced you that your dream isn't realistic or someone else's might be better. When you let other people have more power over your choices than you do, you will end up living for them and not for yourself.

Now, this is not to say that wise counsel is unnecessary nor am I saying that insight from friends and family is useless. Wise counsel is essential to have in your life as it can give you guidance that you may not be able to give yourself.

Insight from friends and family is helpful when it contributes to your growth. But when this advice from others starts to steer you away from your hearts desires, it becomes a serious issue. So serious that it could cause you to never become the person you were created to be or accomplish the things you are meant to accomplish.

Something I want to note is that not all of us are called to be in the limelight! I've heard so many people speak on the topic of purpose as if our purpose must be a profession that brings forth great monetary benefits – and that's absolutely false.

Firstly, living out our purpose will naturally bring forth provision – so chasing money will always be an endless endeavor that serves no purpose to our lives. Secondly, living out our purpose has nothing to do with how popular or rich we become! But it has everything to do with how useful and positively influential we can be for those around us.

What I mean by that is while we are all destined to do incredible things, each of us have a distinct calling unique to us that require us to do different things. Some people are indeed meant to live out their purpose on a platform that reaches thousands of people. And others are meant to use their purpose on a personal level for the service of those who may feel invisible or unimportant.

There are individuals who give guidance to millions of people at a time and positively change lives; which is an incredible accomplishment! But there are those of us who also volunteer at shelters or a community organization on a weekly basis and connect with people who didn't think anyone cared about them.

Whether you cater to the masses and get praised for it or you attend to the underdogs when no one is looking, fulfilling your purpose is priceless and no amount of money compensates for that feeling.

As the original owner of your dream, take pride in the gifts that have been placed inside of you. Commit to executing all of the ideas and plans inside of your head. If you don't do it, who will? There is nothing or no one who can steal your dream from your heart. Sure, someone else may aspire to do the same thing as you, but they'll never do it exactly like you because no one on this earth is exactly like you. You're it!

We do so much in this life out of obligation. We love our spouses because we feel obligated to be good spouses. We're there for our friends at three o'clock in the morning even when we have a long day ahead of us because we feel obligated to be good friends. But why don't more of us feel obligated to chase our dream and enhance our own lives?

That fire in our hearts that pulls us in no matter where we are or who we're around is considered our calling. It's what was placed inside of us by our creator and is meant to give our life here on Earth significance and direction. Our calling is an assignment waiting to be completed and a lot of us are procrastinating as if our due date isn't approaching!

We look at our calling as optional when it's actually the exact opposite. It is mandatory that we accomplish what we were born to do!

It's easy for people to tell you who or what to be when they don't have to deal with everything that comes along with it themselves. That is the main reason you should always do what you feel is best for you – because you are the only one who lives with every decision you make.

I remember the first time in my life that I had to make a choice between what I felt others wanted me to do and what I knew to be best for me at that time – and they were two totally different choices.

I went right off to college at the age of seventeen years old. Being the adamant teenager I was, I went in as a freshman knowing exactly what I wanted to study and had projected exactly how long it would take me to complete that chapter of my life before embarking onto phase two: Law School. It didn't take long before I realized I couldn't control every aspect of my life and I was struck for the very first time by what we call life's curveballs. While I'll dive into the specifics in a later chapter, I will say this: My junior year of college would be the last year I spent at the University that became my home-away-from-home. I had to choose to either stay at the university or take some time off and return home.

Against popular opinion and convention, I chose to return home. I knew to expect critique and lectures from those who "expected more from me". But I also knew that removing myself from an unsatisfactory situation would put me in a better place to become who I expected myself to be, not anyone else.

I was hesitant to leave college temporarily in fear of me never returning. But I knew better than to give up and stop trying. I had made it too far! It took making the conscious decision to hold onto my vision and trust the process for me to stay motivated and optimistic about what I could accomplish. No matter if my current situation said otherwise, I knew that my future was worth investing in and my dream was worth pursuing. And the exact same goes for you!

POSITIVE VIBES ONLY

Have you ever heard someone say you are what you eat? People use that expression to describe how you're affected by what you let inside of you. The same goes for your surroundings. You are affected by what you are exposed to.

If you are serious about taking steps towards living your dream, you cannot afford to put yourself in positions that have potential to knock you backwards ten steps. You should treat your dream something like your very own baby. There should be nothing that can separate you from your goals and you have to be willing to protect your dream at any cost - including removing yourself from any negative and toxic environments. This can be a difficult task for many people for many different reasons.

If you've been alive long enough, you know that your relationships with people can either make or break you. Now, whether the relationship makes or breaks you completely depends on what type of relationship you have with that person. There are healthy relationships that bring out the best in you, and there are unhealthy relationships that bring out the very worst in you.

If it's hard for you to differentiate the two, here's an example: Let's say that you have a best friend that you've known for years. This friend is fundamentally a good person in your eyes, but they make so many bad decisions that

most times drag you into troubled situations -
and if they're not putting you into troubled
situations, they're gossiping or instigating some
sort of drama that leaves you in a bad mood.

Along with bad moods comes a lack of
determination to get work done and your
attitude is so negative that all you focus on is
the bad things going on around you instead of
focusing on the good. When you're thinking this
way, you are hindering yourself and putting all
of your plans to work towards greatness on
hold. This kind of friendship serves you no
purpose and it for sure is not going to help you
reach your full potential - if anything, it will hold
you back.

There are so many stories of potentially gifted people that never lived out their potential because they got caught up with the wrong people who clouded their vision. It's so easy to get distracted and caught up in "the now" but we have to realize that what we do *now* drastically affects our *future*.

When it comes to our decisions, there's a domino effect that takes place. A consequence follows every decision we make. It's important to learn the difference between "living **in** the now" and "living **for** the now".

Living in the now means that you don't take the present for granted. You realize every minute of life is a gift and it's important to cherish every moment you're given. Living for the now means you make decisions based on the present without giving any thought to how it could possibly affect your future - for the good and bad. Make sure you're living in the now, but responsibly planning for the future.

Some people should be left where we met them - in our past. It sounds harsh, but it's true. Everybody we meet can't go where we are headed. Not everyone is equipped to support you the whole way through your journey. Most people we meet serve a temporary purpose in our lives. We meet them, learn something from them, remember them, but don't keep them around forever.

Of course this advice is easier said than done. We spend valuable time building bonds and memories with the very individuals that I'm suggesting we leave behind! But here's a truth that we need to shed light on: Given the circumstance, it is okay to be selfish. It's common for us to worry about other people's feelings more than our own, but that doesn't make it right.

Perhaps there is someone you know who continues to bring negative energy around you and you're fed up with their conversations and actions. Before you select them for elimination, think about whether or not you have stood up for yourself and verbalized your frustration. If they don't know how their behavior negatively affects you, it certainly won't change. Have a talk with them that expresses where you are in your life, what you're trying to do, and what you need from them as your friend.

A real friend will listen to you, hear you, and try to better the friendship so that you ultimately can thrive.

However, if you've had the talk and nothing changes then it's time to get selfish. Someone who disregards your needs and wants is someone who will always put themselves before you. A selfish friend is no friend at all! There's no shame in surrounding yourself with love, support, and positivity - as well as there being no shame in getting rid of those who *can't* provide love, support, or positivity.

All of the negative vibes that come along with the not-so-good relationships can be detrimental to your growth as an individual and definitely a hindrance in your journey. It is your job to make sure that your so-called friends are being true friends to you.

Real friends not only bring out the positivity inside of us, but they encourage us and push us to do our best no matter what. If the relationship you have with someone doesn't contribute to your growth and give you inspiration to be all that you can be, then it's not a relationship worth having.

You have to make it a priority to put yourself in positive environments at all times. Will there sometimes be arguments? Yes. Will there be some bad vibes even between positive people? Absolutely. But these circumstances should only and always be momentarily. Being around negative people will turn you into a negative person. Whereas being around positive people with great energies will enhance the positivity within you.

The last thing you want to do is surround yourself with individuals that are afraid of change because that could possibly influence you to be fearful of the change you so desperately need. They may not come out and say "you should be scared of change!" but they will definitely find something discouraging to say about every single thing you do in pursuit of chasing your dreams.

Influence is one of the strongest forces we deal with on a daily basis from everyone we're around, so it's vital that you remain aware of who and what you allow to be an influence in your life.

Depending on where we are or what we're doing, being around negativity is inevitable due to the fact that we can only control our own attitudes and no one else's. When we find ourselves in situations that are out of our control, remember to influence the situation - not be influenced by the situation. Try your best to shed light on the positivity that everyone else is ignoring at that moment. Not only does this effort empower you in that situation, it also will help those around you to challenge their position and consider viewing things through your positive lens.

It's significantly important to surround yourself with people that understand and support your vision. Trying to figure out what exactly you want to do with your life and how to go about it is intricate enough, the last thing anyone in that position needs is someone around them questioning their every move.

Remove yourself from the clutter of negativity and surround yourself with peace, understanding, and mutual support! Who you have in your corner cheering you on makes all the difference in how strong you become mentally throughout this journey of following your dream. Only a few people will make it to the end of your journey with you, and that's when you will find out who your real friends are.

I think the issue of the internet being such a determining factor in creating positive and negative attitudes deserves a little attention. We become so consumed by what others are doing that we are distracted from our personal responsibilities.

It could be something as simple as scrolling past a picture on our phones of someone else and seeing someone who *appears* to have it all together compared to how we view ourselves! I remember seeing a selfie of a woman I was friends with on a social media site. In this picture she appeared to have clear skin, beautiful hair, and perfect teeth as she obviously was sitting in a brand new car on a hot summer's day!

Instantly I was overcome with jealousy and dissatisfaction. Being someone who has struggled with acne for years, I automatically accused her of manipulating her followers with filters to make her skin look perfect – simply because my skin wasn't. I couldn't help but notice how effortlessly her hair laid on her shoulders and I couldn't think of the last time I had a good hair day! And how was she so young with a new luxurious car? Seriously?

I might as well have asked myself why I couldn't be her all together. My mood was affected for the remainder of that day because I allowed what someone posted make me feel like I couldn't measure up. That's not okay. I let someone else's shine dim my light - and that's unacceptable.

That scenario happened to me a few times before I made the decision to disconnect myself from the internet temporarily and intentionally work on "liking" myself genuinely as much as I liked things about other people.

It may sound extreme to some, or even dramatic. But to me, self-acceptance is that serious. The moment I realized I held others in higher esteem as I did myself I knew something needed to be done to nip that in the bud. I made it a point to acknowledge my flaws, face them, and embrace them in the comfort of my own privacy and pace! And once I accomplished that task, I was able to exude true confidence no matter how brightly the person next to me shined!

Now that I've addressed how we should deal with individuals that may intimidate us from time-to-time, I thought it'd be fitting to also address the individuals that may not intimidate us at all! There are many things about my generation that bother me on a daily basis, but one of the most annoying things has to be how much "haters" are referenced and acknowledged!

Some people can't post one picture without giving a shout out to their haters or *thanking* their haters for giving them the motivation to "do what they do" (whatever that is). And most recently "haters" are being asked the same question repeatedly, "Are you mad?"!

I want to firstly address what people consider haters to be: Someone who is jealous of others and their accomplishments and rather than giving them credit for being awesome, they act as if they like nothing about that person out of pure jealousy!

Now that we all understand what a "hater" is, I want to elaborate on why it's pathetic to thank them for anything at any time. There's nothing truer than someone's actions speaking louder than their own words. You're saying that you're not phased by your haters, but by giving them a shout out every chance you get your actions are saying the exact opposite.

If you truly were not concerned with what others had to say about you then they would be non-existent in your life; and most importantly non-existent in your daily thoughts! Why thank someone who has done nothing for you? Why ask if anyone is mad about your life when their opinion means nothing to you?

When someone that dislikes you sees that they're being mentioned in every post you upload, they know that they control a portion of your mind! They know that even though you say you're "unbothered", what they say and do indeed bothers you. Don't give them that satisfaction!

Instead of thanking our haters for motivating us, we need to thank ourselves for being self-motivated to make the moves that got us to where we are. Instead of asking our haters if they're mad or not, we need to ask ourselves are we truly happy? We all have had a hater or two, but let them do their job and make sure you're doing your job - which is succeeding without acknowledging them!

GOT CONFIDENCE?

There are many things that people say you need in order to follow your dream - money, time, and a plan just to name a few. But one thing that a lot of people fail to mention is having confidence.

In order for you to decide that your dream is worth pursuing, you first have to believe that you are worth investing in! If you don't believe in yourself, how will you promote your idea? How will you sell your vision if you don't believe you're capable?

The very first thing you have to do - before writing a plan, before networking, and even before telling friends and family about your goals - is believe that you can and will do what it is you see yourself doing. If you don't have confidence in your own ability, then all of the work you put into executing your plan will likely be unsuccessful.

The power of confidence will convince others to believe in you as well. When you possess an assertiveness about yourself, you can tell someone about your goals and your plans to achieve them with nothing written on paper, no money in the bank, and not have one professional relationship and whoever you tell will believe that you'll find a way to make this dream come true despite of what currently stands against you.

People being in agreement with you is the response that confidence can demand if only you embody it and allow it to flow out of you.

So how do you get to the point where you are fully confident and ready to take on the world? You have to take time to evaluate yourself in depth. This means you'll have to face the things about yourself that you either dislike or are uncomfortable with as you attack the insecurity head-on!

Being confident doesn't mean you only like a few things about yourself but you act as if your flaws don't exist in hopes of them magically disappearing on their own! That's not going to happen. You can't deal with or heal from something that you won't acknowledge.

Be honest with yourself and uncover your hidden insecurities.

Whether your weakness is public speaking, lack of resilience - or anything along the lines of not being sure about yourself - the issue has to be dealt with so that you don't stand in your own way of following your dreams!

When you keep your insecurities hidden, you become its prisoner. There are places your insecurities say you can't go. There are things that your insecurities say you can't do; and you believe every word.

From this moment on, your insecurities have no more power over your mind! It's time for you to tell your insecurities where you will go and what you will do. It's also time that you tell them where they cannot live - and that's within you!

You have something so necessary to offer the world and so many people are looking forward to experience a gift like the one that lies within you and there's no time to let negative feelings slow you down!

We all have insecurities at some point of our lives. It's important to know that you're not alone in feeling uncertain about yourself sometimes. It is common for things to happen that cause us to stop in our tracks and question our decisions and abilities. However, it's not a good thing when we let those situations shut us down permanently.

You're going to encounter detours on this journey - meaning everything is not going to go perfectly. Not every meeting, interview, or social event you attend will run smoothly! I'm not telling you this to discourage you, but to encourage you to prepare for the learning process!

There will be professionals that know from the moment you walk into a room that you are not an expert in your field, but they do want to know how confident you are in your ability to dominate that field.

You won't have the answer to every question you're asked. Or you won't have the solution to every problem you face. But you can choose to rise to the occasion as you confidently display why you want this opportunity, and more importantly, why the professionals should want you! Even experts make mistakes and are forced to revise and re-do - I mean they're humans just like us - so don't beat yourself up about not being perfect!

I urge you to learn how to evaluate the mistakes you make and learn something valuable from each of them to help your development as an individual and professional.

The fear of rejection has been something that has stopped us from doing things since our childhood. We all had that crush we were afraid to talk to because we didn't want to be embarrassingly rejected. But as adults, we can't afford to let a "what if" mindset stop us from going after "what could be".

Not everyone will understand your vision right away. Some people are going to tell you no or "not this time around". But guess what? That doesn't have to mean that your journey has come to a dead end! If you let a few no's stop you from making it happen, you simply don't want it bad enough.

One of the best ways to thrive in this specific area is to try and not take the rejection you receive personally. Being told no, or not quite does not mean that your dream is silly and you're a worthless human being. It means that this is not the place for you or the right time - that's it. Don't rip yourself apart over something that is meant to build you up! Let these obstacles build your muscle.

While having a support system - that can be as small as one dependable person in your life - is very important, it's not as important as you believing in yourself.

Imagine yourself standing at one end of a tightrope high up in the air with your support system standing behind you cheering you on to walk to the other side. You can hear their encouraging chants: "You're so brave!" "You can do it!" "We've got your back!", as you look ahead to the other end of the tightrope. It looks so far away from where you're standing. What if you stumble? What if you stop midway through because of fear?

At this point, you've blocked the screams from your support system out and all you can hear now are the discouraging thoughts of your own. Your thoughts are so loud and so scary that you consider not going through with it. But then something happens! A still, yet powerful, voice in your head speaks over the now quiet discouragements and tells you that it's worth a shot to try and walk the tightrope. That assertive and confident voice goes on to tell you that you may have to walk the tightrope slowly, but you'll certainly make it to the other side and you'll be so happy and proud that you did! Imagine yourself choosing to believe.

You've now chosen that you are brave enough to walk that tightrope. You've decided to make it to the other side instead of walk away from it.

The vision of the tightrope experience is analogous to you choosing to silence the negative voices in your head and pursue your dream. As important as it is to have someone on your side rooting for you, that alone does not determine whether or not you'll ever make it to your dream destination - just like not having someone to support you shouldn't stop you from walking towards your goal. **You are the deciding factor**!

There comes a time when you have to block out all of the voices that surround you - whether they be positive or negative - and find it in yourself to believe that you indeed are capable of following your dream no matter how far away the ending goal seems to appear.

Be more eager to achieve your goals than you are to walk away from them. You may stumble. It may not happen as quickly as you'd like. But it will happen, if only you choose to confidently walk across that tightrope.

I'm aware that making the decision to silence the negative thoughts is a lot easier said than done for most of us. Some of us have been told repeatedly how much of a joke it is to chase a dream. Maybe someone has told you that you're incapable of accomplishing anything, let alone make your dream life your very own reality.

I want to point out something very important about the kind of people that speak so negatively to others; if and when someone talks down on your ideas, goals, and aspirations, their aim is to empower themselves by tearing you down the best way they know how.

I don't have to know you personally to know that whatever that negative individual says about you or to you is a lie! The discouraging and disrespectful comments that come out of these kinds of people's mouths say nothing about you, but says everything about them!

People that are full of fear and insecurities can only feel powerful if they see someone else feeling lower than them. Don't ever fall for such a vicious plan. In order to tear something down it has to be standing up. Therefore, when others try to kill your spirit, it's because they see how lively and powerful you can potentially be! Sometimes others see the potential in us before we see it within ourselves. Remember that!

PRACTICE PATIENCE

To be honest with you for a moment, I'm purposely writing this chapter during a time that I am struggling with being patient. When you have a clear vision of what it is that you want to do and where you want to be, it becomes difficult to take little steps in order to get to that place.

There's an urge in us that wants to skip the small, not-so-fun details and just get to our dream life already! But something I am reminding myself of daily - specifically by writing this chapter during a time in which I'm feeling the exact opposite - is that the chapter of my life I'm currently in is preparing me for the next one and the same goes for you! Where you are in your life right now - no matter how good or bad it may feel - is preparing you for the next phase of your life that will require you to use the lessons you're learning now. Everything that goes on in this current phase will teach you something that you will be able to take into the next phase as it'll be a tool you can use for future victories.

You may be at a point where nothing is happening according to your plan and you're frustrated to say the very least. No matter what you do or how hard you try you can't seem to move forward and you don't understand why. If this circumstance is relatable to you in any way, you're most likely in a season that's designed to help you master patience. None of us like to hear this while we're going through it, but you must realize how valuable and crucial this lesson is concerning your journey.

Practicing patience allows you to enable your dream to develop in its entirety. If you rush this process, you'll end up with a premature product. And if you rush this season, you'll live your entire life watching the clock as you're distracted from the beauty that's surrounding you in this very moment.

There is a constructive lesson to be learned in *everything* that we go through. As difficult as it is to reflect on what you should be learning during a time of trials, it's important to at least try to figure out what your season could be teaching you. Learning from the trying times will change your life and help your personal and professional growth in ways that you never imagined – but only if you allow it to.

This time of your life is the one of most beneficial and defining periods. You will either let this season of mastering patience make you stronger or break you down. Don't let the road blocks placed in front of you convince you that you'll never complete the journey.

There will be times that you feel as though your pursuit to make your dream a reality is failing, but that's simply **F**alse **E**vidence **A**ppearing to be **R**eal! The only way you'll be sure to fail is if you give up during the process and walk away. Time being delayed and plans changing does not make you a failure, nor does it make your goal impossible to reach. You must proceed if you want to succeed! If all dreams were obtainable within a few months with no stress, challenge, or sacrifice required, everyone would do it.

During this time of impatience and doubt, we're more likely to grow envious of those around us that "seem" to have it all together. It could be anybody from your best friend to a celebrity that you follow on social media. The comparison that you make between you and the individual has the power to diminish your confidence and leave you drowning in jealousy.

The first thing to note is being on the outside looking in on someone else's life never gives you the full image. There are things that go on in other people's lives that we will never know about - and if we did, we sure wouldn't envy it.

Everyone is fighting to become who they're meant to be, even when we don't see the battle wounds that are most likely internal. The second thing to note is that you deserve to give yourself credit.

There are hundreds of people out there who are established and well-off, but that doesn't take away from your efforts or potential one bit! It's unfair and inaccurate to compare your chapter one to someone else's chapter ten.

It's okay to admire someone else for their accomplishments as long as you don't discredit your worth and potential as a result of it. If you find yourself in a discouraging or doubtful mood when others seem to be further ahead of you (By the way, I have definitely been there before), find someone who is thriving in the field you want to pursue and use them and their story as inspiration! Pay attention to their work ethic and look for any patterns in their business decisions. That way you're doing two important things that can help your growth as an individual and a professional:

1- You're exposing yourself to success through a lens that shows you some of the key aspects of becoming and remaining successful in your field.

2- Your mindset will shift from "who cares if they've done more than I have?" to "because they are a few steps ahead of me, I can learn something from them!"

Our attitude is a small thing that makes a huge difference in our behavior and decisions. As I mentioned before, it takes a daily reminder for me to stay patient and focused on my path and no one else's. If we could all wake up one morning and instantly be living our dream, we would do just that. Unfortunately, it doesn't work that way and it takes a lot more work than we initially think.

The important thing to remember is that however long your traffic jam seems to be, the time will pass and the red or yellow light will eventually turn green. And it is much wiser to let the time pass as you press forward through all of the obstacles than to completely give up on something you truly want and deserve.

It's both easy and common to get discouraged because the life you're living now doesn't even come close to the life you know you deserve. There are so many times that I think to myself "This can't be all that I'm meant to do". This feeling of dissatisfaction sinks in as we begin to feel bad about our life's current circumstances. Then we start to think about what we wish our life was like or where we wish we could be as if these desires are impossible to accomplish.

Recently, I've learned to overcome these feelings of dissatisfaction by planning! I know you're probably thinking about how in the world the two could correlate. Let me explain exactly what I mean! When I have days that I feel unfulfilled in any way, I begin to feel sorry for myself or doubt my decisions. This mentality is unhealthy for anyone at any time in their life, but especially when you're trying to achieve a goal. So I started to take those dreary days and use them to plan.

Whatever it is that I'm feeling bad about is what I plan for. Let's say you want to start a business but you're at a total stand-still in your pursuit due to lack of finances and you're feeling pretty down about it. What you would do in this situation is get a pen and some paper and jot down what it is that needs to happen in order for you to get the ball rolling!

Maybe a bank turned you down when you asked for a loan - your next step would be to put on paper the work you need to do to possibly better your chances of getting the loan the next time around.

Maybe your issue isn't that technical and you want to do something like start your own clothing line, but you're not sure about what style of clothes you want to design. You could spend some free time to go to some local clothing stores in your area and take note of what designs jump out at you as you browse around the store. Now, your dream may have nothing to do with either example I gave but the concept within them goes for every dream out there.

These moments are what I call "traffic-jams". As the issues approach, they cause you to slow down and sometimes bring you to a complete stop. But the key is to be patient during this time so that you not only learn to master patience, but you also give your dream the time it needs to develop into the successful venture you and I both know it can be.

Our road to success will have detours and traffic jams along the way, but if we really want what we're working towards then we will be patient enough to sit through the traffic and wait the issue out as we trust that the road will clear up eventually.

SHIFTING GEARS

Not everyone decides to start their journey right away as they follow their dream early on in life. Not to mention the unexpected plot twists that life throws at us that take our focus off of our dream momentarily. We live pretty stable, planned out, well-functioning - but not perfect - lives and we have been doing so for years. We do what we have to do to pay the bills and we're accepting of this (note I didn't say "happy with this").

While it's great to have a means of provision for ourselves and our loved ones, leading a life of "getting by" lacks passion - which is one of the most important things we need in order to pursue our dreams.

Once we're settled into our own ways of contentment and the acceptance of "good enough", we have thoughts similar to "this has been my life's routine so far, why change it now?" Or we convince ourselves that it's too late for any kind of dream chasing.

If these thoughts have crossed your mind at any point, ask yourself this question: If it's too late to follow my dream, then why is that desire still burning inside of my heart? The answer to that question is simple: As long as you are alive, you still have time to go after whatever it is that your heart and mind can't forget about.

I was doing some thinking the other day and I can't seem to stop thinking about this specific word: **contentment**. By definition, contentment means being in a state of happiness and satisfaction. However, I can't help but to question that definition. Does being content really mean you're happy? Or does it mean you're comfortable? Now, some will argue that being happy and comfortable are one in the same. But I want to address this in a specific way.

In regards to our lives, a lot of us would say we're "content" with where we are in life. No, everything is not perfect but things could be worse, so you're content! Right? I agree, things could be worse. But I will also argue that things could be better as well and I'm not sure if contentment encourages "better"!

We become so immune to doing the same things just on different days that we confuse being happy with just being comfortable with our lives. Just because you don't hate your life doesn't mean that you love your life! And shouldn't we all be madly in love with our life? I don't know about you but I know that I want to be madly in love with every moment of mine!

When we become comfortable with our lives, we don't desire growth or change. Being comfortable on a couch is heaven on a rainy day! Being comfortable around a friend is needed in order to truly be yourself - **but being comfortable with your life is different!**

When you're content with your life, you don't see any reason to change anything because you like things the way that they are. While that mentality is better than hating everything about your life, it's important to remember something. **_We should never stop learning because life never stops teaching!_** If we are content with how things are that means our routines and thought processes are the same day in and day out! What is that lifestyle teaching us? In what ways can you grow from repeating the same thing with the same people every day? There are none. And we miss out on life's greatest lessons when we run from change.

Whether it's your job, your relationship or even the city that you live in, don't let your life pass you by without making the personal decision to live in happiness instead of contentment. Being comfortable is safe, and stepping out of your comfort zone to pursue true happiness is a risk; we all know that, but *we shouldn't live in fear* of that!

Happiness is something that everyone should feel in their lifetime, especially you. You know exactly what it is that would make you the happiest you've ever been! You've been wanting it for a while, but you've also been running from it for just as long! Please stop running from it & run towards it! You deserve to know what happiness genuinely feels like.

You and I both know that somewhere deep down inside of you there is an urge to follow your heart and achieve that grand goal, but the idea of leaving a life of stability to start on a road of uncertainties terrifies you - and you're not sure if abandoning what you know to be most comfortable or familiar is worth the risk.

Perhaps you've already begun your quest to your dream success, but something happened unexpectedly that led to you having to stop in your tracks for the time being. What if our dream is in one direction but we've established our life in the opposite direction? How do we make that transition without losing faith and gaining fear? The solution is more simplistic than we think.

We all have different individual strengths and weaknesses. But one strength that every one of us have the ability to withhold is resilience. The refusal to give up on yourself is what will be the foundation of your success story. Here you have the life that you live, and in your heart lives the life you wish to create. The task now becomes bridging the gap between the two! While this task certainly won't be easy, neither is it impossible.

Shifting gears doesn't always mean immediately jumping from your current situation to your ideal situation. Often times we have to firstly change our attitudes about the process we'll have to go through in order to get to our ideal situation.

As difficult as it may be for most of us, we have to mentally accept that it may take more time than we initially thought to accomplish some goals. It's important to accept this possibility so that we aren't totally overwhelmed and upset when the time is passing us by and we seem to be going nowhere fast! I feel like I'm raining on a parade for telling you to expect something to go wrong, but it's too common not to address!

Often times people will attempt to achieve a goal and quit after their first attempt because of failure or an unexpected outcome! That's where having the expectations of curve balls become helpful! If we prepare ourselves for a change of plans, we can evaluate how to go about achieving that goal differently next time – rather than giving up right away when it doesn't work the first time around.

I think we all know and understand that making your hearts desires your reality is not an overnight experience. There will be times that your efforts appear to fail. Trial and error may become the story of your life for a little while. And people may not understand anything about what you have going on, but it's your job to trust yourself and more importantly the process.

A lot of people would call me a fool (and probably wanted to when I told them) for taking a break from college to work full-time. All I heard when I started as a freshman was "It's great that you're going right off! Now go on through until you graduate!" While that was the plan and would have been ideal, that's not what worked for me! I had to make the challenging and mature decision to change my path a little in order to get back on track – and I trust that this path will lead me exactly where I need to be.

Had I not trusted myself, I would've let other people's assumptions that I'd never go back to college have power over my life and I'd still be in the dark place I removed myself from. If you don't trust yourself other people will make you doubt yourself. And if you don't trust the process of building the foundation that your dream will stand on, you'll fold under pressure and quit before you see any benefits of working so hard.

It was only a year ago that I was packing my things to go and begin my fourth year as an undergrad studying Political Science. I was so excited to be so close to graduation and even closer to the "next phase" of my life! I had been researching law schools, involved in extracurricular activities to keep my passion for law strong and sharp, and most importantly I was extremely confident that my initial plan would fall through. I mean, what could go wrong?

Well I soon found out that *life* can go wrong and it has no problem with interrupting your plans and steering you in a new and unexpected direction.

At the beginning of my academic school year I received a check with leftover funds from my financial aid that covered my college expenses. I opened the envelope and stared at the total amount as I mentally panicked about how this was the only source of income I depended on and it was close to nothing. I was currently unemployed and I didn't have a car – which made the job search more difficult because I was limited to how far away from my campus I could work! My parents weren't able to send me monthly allowances and because I knew how my family struggled financially at times, I didn't have the heart to call and ask for a lump sum of money to hold me.

In a matter of a couple of weeks the thought of my fourth year in college went from the happiest time of my life, to the most challenging time of my life. And to my surprise, it was only going to get worse.

Five months into the fall semester, I found out that I was pregnant. At this point, I'd found a job working in retail part-time (which required daily prayer in itself) which wasn't even paying half of the bills, and was trying my hardest to stay positive and motivated to do well in school full time - and now this? Aside from me humiliating my family and having gone against my religious upbringing, I still had no car, no health insurance that would cover my doctor's visits and now not an ounce of energy or positivity in my body.

Thanks to a ton of prayer, tears, and support from my very close friends and family, I'd eventually come around to the idea of becoming a mother in spite of that not being anywhere in my plans. But three weeks after I found out I was pregnant, severe bodily complications and several hospital visits revealed that I had lost my baby and a piece of my heart forever. It was the morning after my loss that I was scheduled to go into work. Because the campus transportation didn't run on the weekends, I had to walk for thirty-five minutes to get there on time during the month of January, in the state of Michigan. All the while I'm expected to show up for work, show up for class, and thrive at everything. It was a lot and it was hard.

My body had never been through so many physical pains and changes before then. My mind had never been so mentally drained and weary. I needed to heal and recover from everything! And in order to do that, I had to make the choice to pause everything and back track a little.

I decided to move home with my family, who thankfully welcomed me with open arms, and found a full-time job so that I could save for a car and my own apartment. I explained to them that I needed about six months off from school and then I'd resume pursuing my degree once some things were taken care of, and luckily, they approved.

Currently? I'm three months into the six I gave myself to save and I'm working full-time at a factory as a metal inspector. Glamorous, right? Because I went right off to college at seventeen years old, it's been hard to adjust to not being in school at all – especially now that I'm so close to graduating.

When I made the decision to take a break from school I knew it was what I needed to do, but that didn't do anything for the embarrassment I felt. I knew how many people were anxious to see me graduate later this year. I knew that I should have been applying to law schools instead of applying to work full-time at a factory! I couldn't believe that when folks from my hometown would see me hanging around town I would have to tell them I'd be hanging around for a little while longer. This wasn't my plan! However, it took time for me to realize that after everything I'd been through previously, I needed this time to build myself back up into the strong and driven individual that I was before life threw the curve ball my way!

I refuse to discredit my efforts by comparing my journey to someone else's. Just like they don't know what I've gone through to get to this point, I don't know what they've gone through! We all are fighting our own battles that require different techniques to win.

When I worked in retail, I worked my butt off every day because I knew I needed that job to help me live on my own and I took pride in it. Now that I'm working in manufacturing, I work my butt off every day because I know I need the money for my car and apartment - and I take pride in that. And I'm working my butt off through this season of transition because I know I need these tools for the next season of my life, and I take a great amount of pride in that! I'm not letting my "traffic jam" stop me in any way.

I got off of work at seven o'clock this morning, got a few hours of sleep, and I'm writing this chapter before I go into work tonight. I'm not going to work eight hours for a company every day and not put any time into working towards my own dreams! My story doesn't end here, and neither should yours.

VICTIM VS VICTOR

It's important to keep in mind that the obstacles that we encounter are placed in our lives to strengthen us, not stop us! Trust me, I know all too well how it feels to feel defeated and uninspired. Those feelings are understandable when everything around you is crumbling before your eyes and none of your plans are even close to going as planned. But do you want to know the good news? No matter what happens to us, we have the power within us to turn every situation around for our benefit!

We only have control when we see obstacles through a lens that says this happened for me rather than to me. We're going to examine a character named Vicky. I'm going to give two analogies on how being a victim and victor both affect us differently and why it's important to choose one over the other!

The Story of Vicky the Victim

It was the day before Vicky's big presentation! She had done her research, studied the concepts, and had her oral exam all written up. Everything seemed to be ready to go, except her confidence. Vicky kept replaying the same scenario in her mind over and over again. Her professor would call her name assertively as she began to feel small drops of sweat grow strong and big enough in order to fall down her body creating the most uncomfortable tickle down her back. Trying to control her visibly shaking hands, Vicky would then attempt to recite her oral exam in front of everyone - but nothing would come out! She would forget everything as if she had not prepared at all! How humiliating would that be?

In efforts to make sure she wouldn't fall on her face in front of her peers, she tried reciting her speech to herself in the mirror over and over again so that her memory wouldn't let her freeze on presentation day! Although she could have asked a friend to watch her do it and act as an audience, she didn't want to embarrass herself in any way, so she stayed to herself and practiced all night in front of her mirror!

The morning of her exam had finally arrived and Vicky couldn't have felt any more prepared! She had every word memorized and felt as though she was prepared to answer any questions that her professor or peers may have asked! On her way to class Vicky eased her mind by reminding herself that she did just fine in her room, so she'd be just fine in the classroom too!

It was finally time for Vicky to present! Unfortunately, what she'd anticipated to be a breeze quickly became the humiliating struggle she had feared all along! Everything that she practiced escaped her mind and was replaced with the intimidation of an entire lecture hall full of students staring at her in a way that made her feel like everyone was waiting for her to embarrass herself!

It didn't matter anymore that she had done amazing research and had worked hard at fully understanding the concepts of which she presented. All that mattered was that she was not prepared to present all of her hard work to a crowd of people! Practicing in front of a mirror did nothing for her public speaking skills – and this reality was hitting her at the most inopportune time.

After what seemed like a lifetime, Vicky's ten minute presentation was over and she made the walk of shame back to her seat. She failed and she knew it. Vicky couldn't believe what had just happened to her! That feeling of fear, shame, and incompetence all wrapped into one was something she never wanted to feel again. It was on that day she decided that public speaking was not her "thing" and if she could help it, she'd never do it again.

Once class was over, Vicky rapidly was the first to leave and couldn't wait to go distract herself and forget that the last hour of her life had ever happened!

It's obvious that Vicky felt victimized by her public speaking experience! Having to endure that embarrassment made her feel powerless and incapable. It's likely that from now on, Vicky will become imprisoned by her thoughts that tell her to stay away from any type of public speaking – even though that could mean depriving herself of some amazing opportunities that could open doors for her future! Now let's examine the same scenario, but through a more brave lens.

The Story of Vicky the Victor

It was the day before Vicky's big presentation! She had done her research, studied the concepts, and had her oral exam all written up. Everything seemed to be ready to go, except her confidence. Vicky kept replaying the same scenario in her mind over and over again. Her professor would call her name assertively as she began to feel small drops of sweat grow strong and big enough in order to fall down her body creating the most uncomfortable tickle down her back. Trying to control her visibly shaking hands, Vicky would then attempt to recite her oral exam in front of everyone - but nothing would come out! She would forget everything as if she had not prepared at all! How humiliating would that be?

In efforts to make sure she wouldn't fall on her face in front of her peers, she tried reciting her speech to herself in front of her mirror. Because she wanted to prepare as best as she could, she asked a friend to come over and watch her present to act as an audience! Vicky and her friend went over the presentation time and time again before they called it a night!

The morning of Vicky's exam was finally here! She walked into the lecture hall feeling completely prepared – that is until her nerves began to build as it got closer to her turn! Shockingly, Vicky choked during her presentation even though she used her friend for practice! Turns out speaking in front of one person is way different than speaking in front of forty people. She forgot key points and had trouble making eye contact with the crowd, which were two components that her final grade weighed heavily on.

Feeling ashamed and disappointed in herself, Vicky knew that she never wanted to feel this way or fail that miserably again! She stayed after class to speak to her professor one-on-one and she received great tips on how to improve her preparation and delivery for similar assignments in the future. Vicky also figured if she'd ever get better at public speaking, she'd first better speak to the public more often! Soon thereafter, Vicky took advantage of every public speaking opportunity she could recognize - even if it was as small as volunteering to read a passage from a text book aloud in class! It was decisions like these that

assured Vicky that she would never be ashamed of her

public speaking performance ever again.

While both scenarios started the same way, Vicky's actions created two drastically different outcomes. When we fail or disappoint ourselves, there are two ways to make certain that we never feel that way again: to avoid that experience in the future or to analytically address the experience for the future.

Sure, avoiding a situation that intimidated us in the past prevents us from ever being intimidated again! That's a pretty simple logic to follow. However, avoiding things that have challenged us before also prevents us from allowing that challenge to change us for the better! I'm assuming you're reading this book because something about making a major life change intrigues you. If that's true, following this logic of avoidance is not the way to go.

I think it's safe to say that the theme of this book is to not run away from what scares us! Avoiding any issues or challenges that we face does not make them go away - it puts the issues and challenges on standby until we approach them at a later date. Is that what we want? Do we honestly want to put our fears on hold? Or do we want to face them, put them to rest, and move on?

Analytically addressing our challenges not only helps us grow out of bad habits, but it's an amazing way to learn important things about ourselves. I always say that there is no way you can know what you want out of life if you don't know who you are! Being completely informed about what's within us and being in touch with that information is essential to our pursuit of fulfillment.

The process of getting to know ourselves in depth is so precious and empowering! It's a journey that transforms us into individuals that see the value in every obstacle we face. And it's a journey that transforms us from being a victim of circumstance into victors who become undefeated.

When we look at unfortunate circumstances as happening *to* us, we hand over all control which makes us vulnerable and unable to help ourselves get out of that situation. It's hard to see the good in anything when we feel like we've been defeated. In defeat, the opposing side is the winner which in turn makes you the loser.

On the contrary, looking at an unfortunate circumstance as happening *for* us changes our mindset to see everything as a lesson that was meant to enhance our lives! So whether it's positive or negative, win or lose, we benefit from it because we allow that moment to build our muscle rather than tear us down.

I want to make certain you understand what I mean in terms of "controlling" our circumstances that either makes us a victim or victor! It's not a secret that we have hardly any

wasn't okay and I didn't have control. But I

learned that the quicker you feel that pain,

confusion, and anger - instead of harboring it -

the quicker you heal and move forward.

   True characters were revealed within

those around me! It wasn't until recently that

I'd actually lived through "real situations

out the fake in people". And that

given truth! When you nee

or not they're there

measures they'd g

- shows you how muc

where exactly you stand i

People who can't be there fo

days do not deserve to be includ

of your days. This brings me to my n

control over what happens to us or around us in
our lives! Life is too unpredictable to "figure"
out completely. Therefore, the only thing we
really can control is our reaction to the
unfortunate circumstances we may face!

Just because we experience loss doesn't
make us all losers - and understanding the
difference is pivotal to personal growth. Life
happens. And sometimes it hurts a lot. But the
bright side is that there is a lesson to be learned
in every loss we experience... and here are a few
lessons I gained from losing:

By losing control, I was forced to feel.

Being that I'm a natural born leader; it's difficu
for me to sit and allow something or someo
else to do all of the work without any of

input or assistance. But oftentimes things happen in our lives - whether it is physical, emotional, or financial - that have to take its course on its own, requiring none of our input or assistance!

This was very hard for me to accept, as you can imagine. For the first time in my life, I remember feeling helpless. All I could do was feel. I felt the shock of what I'd known to be my realities turn out to be a fantasy. I felt the confusion of being lied to by someone who'd "earned" my trust. I felt the anger of not understanding why God wouldn't r...

...om such a painful & life-ch...

...al... with not being...

For... first ti...

I gained a renewed appreciation for family. I could write an entire book about my incredible family alone, but it wasn't until recently that I emotionally and physically experienced what the love of family is capable of! The power of love - specifically the power of love from those that God designed just for you - is one that you can only feel in order to understand as it's difficult to easily express through words.

If family ties aren't something you feel that you need, I strongly urge you to reconsider! We all need someone in our corners that are there to solely love us through the good and bad times because it will be those people that love you through the hardest moments of your life - which gives you the strength to push towards the best moments of your life!

And lastly, heartbreak is helpful. We all experience it in various forms. And we all hate it. But I believe we all need it at some point. Heartache is a sobering feeling that forces us to take off those blinding glasses to see something for what it really is rather than believe in a fictitious scenario.

The most hurtful thing is to feel as if you're not good enough for someone or something for whatever reason. But the truth is we'll never be "good enough" for something that isn't meant to be ours at that moment. Don't let heartbreak convince you that you're the problem. Allow that experience to show you what's good for you and what's not - and follow that guidance. Our heart's intuition is hardly ever wrong.

This journey is all about confidently pushing forward until your goals are met! People are going to doubt you, some people are going to appear to be further ahead than you, and everything will not go as planned every time – but none of these situations, or anything similar to it, should be powerful enough to break your focus. Choosing to keep your game plan in perspective at all times will help you make decisions that will better position yourself for success. And making that choice alone will ensure that in everything you face, you'll be victorious!

SACRIFICE BEFORE SUCCESS

Before I dive into what to do when trying to strive for success, I want to clarify what "success" is *and* isn't. Over time this term has been misused by so many people that it is now the most talked about subject - yet it is the least understood. When we hear the word "success" we think of luxurious cars, mansions, and lots of zeros and commas! The last thing we think of is health, self-satisfaction, and humility.

Albert Einstein once said, "Try not to become a man of success, but rather try to become a man of value." I don't think the great Albert Einstein was suggesting that we sit around and do nothing with our lives, as he was a very hard worker himself. However, I believe he was referring to the connotations associated with the term "success" such as the invaluable, disposable, and temporary things of this world that people dedicate their lives to chasing after.

Too often we allow material things to have a hold on us when we don't even have a grip of our true selves. This is not to say that owning nice things is a bad thing – I'm simply saying that we should own material things rather than allow them to own us.

Behind all of the glam, gear, popularity, and money – who are you? If you were stripped from everything that society says you need in order to have value, what would you represent? Having the answers to the questions asked is information we each need to have in order to truly live out our purpose. Until we fully understand and are in tune with what we're designed to do, this journey of dream chasing won't end so well.

A lot of us develop a lifestyle of watching-and-waiting. We watch other people enjoy their life and we wait for it to happen for us as if we have no control over our own lives! We're only allotted so much time here on Earth which makes it vital to use our time wisely and pursue our unique purpose without a watch-and-wait attitude.

Regarding our unique purpose, sometimes it can get overwhelming to think about what our purpose is exactly. This is another word that holds a lot of meaning and is sometimes exaggerated. When we think of what our life's purpose might be, we tend to imagine one grand act or duty we're supposed to perform – and most times, it's not always that precise.

For example, your purpose could simply be to provide comfort and support for children. This doesn't mean that your life revolves around one specific moment where you'll help someone's kid in a drastic way.

This means that any time you're around someone younger than you – whether you're at a community event or the grocery store - something pulls at your heart until you say or do something to make that child feel important and cared for! While that was just an example, that "something" that bugs you inside until you act on it is your purpose.

It's almost like we don't have to find our purpose at all – our purpose finds us! If you find yourself being drawn to something constantly no matter where you are or what you're doing, pay close attention to what that could mean for you.

It's also important to note that while our purpose is our very own, it's given to us so that we can give to others in our own ways. What would be the point of having such a gift if we were the only ones to benefit from it? This is not to suggest that we all go out and start charities and open up shelters. I'm saying that the purpose that has been assigned to you is needed in the world right now, and someone is waiting to receive what you have to offer! Whether the act is big or small, someone out there is counting on it.

Our happiness is often times circumstantial. We say things like "I'll be happy when this happens." Or "I'll be ready for change whenever I get that situated." And before we know it five years have gone by and we've done close to nothing to make our dream our reality due to watching & waiting.

Life is happening whether we enjoy it or not, so why waste a second of it? Just because you aren't surrounded by the beautiful view of the sky from a private jet's window doesn't

mean beauty isn't surrounding you right now –
you just have to find it!

It should be of the utmost importance
for us to build lives of value whether this day in
age promotes that or not! Your genuine
happiness – no matter how it looks to others – is
the greatest success. Because so many of us
view this concept as another term for filthy
rich, we deem ourselves unsuccessful when in
fact we achieve great things every day.

No matter how minor or major the task
may be - when anything we set out to achieve is
completed, *we are successful!* It's important to
know and believe that we define our own
happiness no matter how many people say
otherwise! There's nothing wrong with aiming

for a life of success – just make sure the valuable things make you feel successful!

Now that we've gotten past the "fun" part of planning for our journey that entails coming up with all of the exciting ideas – it's time to shed a little light on the not-so-fun part of beginning the journey: *sacrifice.*

As adults, we all have to make sacrifices at some time or another in our lives when we give up something that we desire in exchange for something considered more valuable! A lot of the times making a sacrifice is the exact opposite of fun. However, something worth noting about doing so is that once you consider the bigger picture and how grand the reward will be when you receive the much more valuable objective, it becomes a little easier to practice.

Sometimes the sacrifices are as little as staying in the house when you could go out instead, but sometimes they're a tad bit more demanding and it will take discipline and courage to make the right decisions. There's a bigger picture that needs to be considered when facing these types of decisions. One way I view this subject is analogous to a race.

After the gun goes off it's up to the runner to start running towards the finish line. Just because that gun goes off doesn't mean the race has begun – the race begins when the runner starts running. And the longer the runner waits to put one foot in front of the other, the longer it'll take to reach that finish line.

Making the choice to begin the quest of fulfilling your purpose works the same way. Just because an idea pops into your head or a desire lies inside of your heart doesn't automatically ensure you'll accomplish anything. You have to begin to move in order to make strides towards your vision. And you'll notice that making these moves don't always feel good. But that's the essence of what making a sacrifice is; choosing to trade a preferred option in for one that will bring more value to you in the long run.

When making decisions of these kinds you can't afford to have an impatient attitude. Your desire to have everything right now has to submit to your self-control that will enable you to possess the right things at the right time instead of having to have it right now. There will be plenty of times that we will need to say no when we want to say yes and we'll have to rely on our self-control to make the right choice.

You cannot succeed without having an understanding of true work ethic. Work ethic is a principle that promotes hard work and efforts that birth favorable results. This principle is one we all have heard of but one that very few of us practice. Having a strong work ethic doesn't mean we do the bare minimum that is required. It means that you go above and beyond what's expected in order to do the absolute best job that you can - even when you don't feel like it or it's not in your best interest!

A key component in practicing work ethic is never losing sight of the vision of success that you've engraved into your mind. In doing this, the vision gives you the strength to push forward when obstacles appear to be slowing you down.

So many of us lack the desire to work above and beyond our capability due to the curse of "getting by". By that I mean most of us are immune to mediocrity. There may not be anything extravagant about our daily routines but our life is good enough to make it to the next day. We work to pay our bills, we spend the entire work week looking forward to the weekend, and we spend our lives waiting for the "right time" to make it better. That is the epitome of mediocrity.

It's time we break the cycle of "getting by" for once and for all! From now on we need to choose greatness over good-enough! It doesn't matter much at all what social or geographic background you come from, who you were raised by or how they raised you! It does, in fact, matter how you use your personal experiences to either continue the same pattern or create a new path. It is an absolute personal choice to not want to push yourself to your fullest capability. But if you want to strive like never before and achieve your dreams –

which I believe you do if you're reading this –
you don't have that choice.

There is no room for "good-enough" when
pursuing your purpose. It has to be all-or-
nothing on this journey! Your purpose will
always require the absolute best of you.

In this day in age, being a leader is one of
the biggest sacrifices that face us constantly. I
say it's a sacrifice because going against popular
opinion and making your own path doesn't
seem to be that beneficial given the way that
society works. Over time self-image and
popularity have become much more important
than self-awareness and purpose.

There appears to be no benefit from
being an individual and following your hearts

desires. Seemingly, following the crowd or current trend looks like the most fun and fulfilling, I know – I experience it as well.

But what social media forgets to show you is that creating a habit of following the masses leads a life of emptiness. You only become full of what it pours into you; and however much is poured into you will surely waste away as soon as that fad dies. And then what? Do we sit around, purposeless and empty, and wait for the new "goal" to surface? It's a draining cycle that promotes a false image of security.

This ties directly to being attached to and obsessed with possessing material things that were never meant to last forever! It's perfectly fine to value the things that we like to do and have, but we should never let those things determine our value. A part of becoming an adult is seeking after material things like a nice car, big house, and so on. I'm not suggesting that you feel ashamed of that. I just want to clarify the role that those material things play in our lives. They were created to assist us in living more convenient lives. We are the owners of these possessions, they don't own us.

Making the choice to not live by the applause of others is a sacrifice all in itself given how popular this lifestyle has become. Living out our purpose in private is just as admirable as doing it publicly. We see famous people living their life to the fullest for the world to see all of the time, and when they do great things for their community and others it's amazing to see. However, I want you to remember that true satisfaction comes from doing things out of the kindness of your heart and not for applause.

The only way you will be able to make the choice to follow in the footsteps that have been predestined specifically for you - and more importantly stand firmly on that path - is if you wholeheartedly believe the reward for doing so will be worth it no matter how big the sacrifice!

USE YOUR TIME WISELY

Regardless of how old you are or where you live, it seems like there is always something more fun we'd rather be doing instead of what we're supposed to be doing at the time!

For example, it's currently a Friday night and I'm in the house drinking wine, and writing. I was invited out but I declined the offer because I know I have a busy next two days coming up and this was really the only night open to finish this chapter of my book.

I could have made an excuse or an empty promise to myself to "finish the chapter tomorrow!", but I am the queen of procrastination and I knew for a fact this chapter wouldn't have been finished until next week sometime if I didn't do it tonight. After the work week I had, a night out on the town with endless drinks and friends would have been ideal – but if I don't start making sacrifices now, when will I?

It comes down to how serious you are about attaining your goal and how far you'll go to attain it! We also have to be as honest as possible with ourselves when it comes to our strengths and weaknesses.

One of my weaknesses is procrastination so I have to make an intentional effort to do what's important before I enjoy my free time - otherwise the important things won't get done! I also get distracted very easily and distractions are something we have to get under control before we can get in our work zone and handle business.

I'll set myself up to do at least three hours' worth of writing and spend almost two hours of that reserved time browsing the internet on my phone! I even have gone as far as sending "Hey! How are you?" text messages to people that haven't heard from me in forever in hopes of starting a deep conversation with a childhood friend that would obviously justify my lack of focus.

In an effort to minimize the clutter around me, I now turn my phone off along with the television and I focus all of my attention on what it is that needs to be done. Something I started incorporating into my work-time is break-time! While it's mandatory that we work hard, it's also important not to burn ourselves out! When we work non-stop we exhaust ourselves to the point where our passion becomes painful – and that should never be the case.

Those of us coming of age in this era know exactly what I mean when I say this generation loves to play follow the leader! Everything is a trend that spreads like wildfire and in no time everyone around the country is connecting through some sort of video challenge.

While being carefree and silly throughout our youth is necessary in order to live a full and healthy life, it's important to keep our "playtime" in check so that we don't devote more time to entertaining others than we spend enriching ourselves by achieving personal goals. It is safe to say that social trends will come, go, and come back again. What we don't get back, however, is time. Don't waste the opportunities you're given that helps you take steps closer to your finish line.

I'm going to be honest, you should expect to feel a little alienated during this time of making sacrifices. You have to understand that very few of your peers are on the same page as you at this moment. A lot of them still believe they "have time" before they need to get serious about their future, so they're doing very little to positively influence it.

You, on the other hand, are wise enough to know how greatly every decision you make impacts your future! So to you, the time to start planning and working hard is now – and you couldn't be more correct.

When everyone else is going left, you may have to go right. If everyone is asleep, you may have to stay awake a little while longer. It all comes along with taking an above average path of pursuing what you were born to do - so naturally you'll have to make above average decisions.

People who live their lives with the "I'll do it tomorrow" mentality don't realize how far ahead they could be if only they did what they said they'd do the first time it crossed their mind! The longer we put our plans on hold, the further back we push our finish line. Visualizing it that way alone makes me want to get my butt moving right now!

It's obviously important to use our time wisely so that we can get work done. But it's also equally important to use some of our time to not work so hard and relax. Our physical and mental health is more important than anything you could name. Being healthy internally has to come first before we can live a healthy life. I know how much easier it is said than done, but I want us to start making time for the things we claim we don't have time for. Schedules get hectic and life gets crazier every day! I get it. But we'll be the ones going crazy next if we don't take some time, and soon, to simply unwind and not think about one responsibility!

I have a few ways that work best for me to give myself this downtime. One of the ways is to have a candle-lit bath with my favorite music. I set up all of my fragrances, candles, and clean pj's as I prepare my mind to be in chill mode for the next hour or so! I don't answer one phone call or respond to one text message during this time. I make myself completely unavailable to the world (I think that's my favorite part).

I make sure I select a playlist of music that revolves around positivity. I purposely stay away from classic R&B music or anything that I know will give me a flashback of a not-so-positive memory that could potentially put me in a bad mood (you know we all have that one song that takes us back to when we were young and dumb). I typically pick songs that I've recently learned and liked that don't really have a connotation attached to it just yet. It's quiet, still, and that relaxing experience lasts for as long as I want it to. It works every time.

Another way I love to have downtime is to go someplace alone and journalize. I don't ever have a specific topic in mind to write about, I just write. Whatever comes from my heart and to my mind goes on my paper.

I write about my dreams, my fears, and my flaws. I write about things I've never talked about aloud and I also write about things I can't talk about enough! There's no one standing over my shoulder judging me or no one around to laugh or point fingers. It's just me in a no-pressure environment that makes it easy for me to be honest with myself. Each journal entry is different but is just as special as the last. They all collectively illustrate me as an individual, and over the years I've been able to watch my growth as I read old notes as if I'm reading a book about someone else!

The act of "letting it all out" in private is very therapeutic for me and it has always eased my mind when I needed that release the most.

While those are examples of how I make time for relaxation, what makes your alone time therapeutic might be drastically different! And that's perfectly fine just as long as we all find what exactly takes us to that vulnerable place!

So far we've established that making time for work and alone time is essential – but there's one more area to cover: playtime! The biggest way to cheat yourself is to not get out and see the beautiful world we live in with the beautiful people that live in it!

Of course it's ideal to book a flight and travel across the globe to some exotic island and experience beauty in its essence. But I'm not just talking about taking a dream trip. I'm mainly referring to finding the beauty and adventure in what's surrounding you right now! Find some restaurants that you've never been to before and invite a friend. Perhaps you could meet someone at a local park and talk a walk – or even exercise! No matter what social preference you have, the point of making room for "playtime" is to strengthen our bonds with others aside from using our phones while making unforgettable memories at the same time!

The internet has us so hooked on connecting in a way that leaves us ultimately disconnected. We're more prone to send a text message rather than make a phone call and we'll FaceTime rather than speak face-to-face! I understand that it is all about convenience these days, but I'd love to see us treat human interaction more like an incomparable experience instead of an inconvenience.

BECOME YOUR POTENTIAL

It's one thing to envision yourself as your best self, but it's another to enact that vision and actually *become* the person you see yourself as. There is no way we can fulfill our purpose entirely if we don't ever actively live out our full potential. This is obviously something that doesn't happen overnight or even over a short span of time. Development and transformations take time for all of us!

Being aware of the potential inside of you and boasting about what you *could* do will only take you so far. I can assure you it certainly won't make all of your dreams magically come true. Talking about what it is you want to accomplish isn't enough – at some point you have to make a move towards that goal in order to get results! Don't allow yourself to become complacent with knowing that "if you really wanted to, you could – but it's too much work, so you won't".

So many people are gifted and equipped to do miraculous things throughout their lifetime but will never experience that fulfillment due to them settling, refusing to work at it or, simply put, fear of failure (please don't be that person).

Why is it that we admire dream-chasers so much, but the moment we have the opportunity to do the same we come up with every excuse not to? As if living out a destiny is only meant for a special type of person and the rest of us are just... here. Whether you know it or not, every single person on this Earth is special enough to live out their destiny. *We are all entitled to that experience*! The issue is not that some individuals are "living the dream" because their luck is just that good. The issue is that so many of us aren't because our drive, dedication, and work ethic is just that bad. Plain and simple!

A lot of us don't like the idea of having to abandon our norm in order to create a new life! Anything "new" scares most of us for many reasons. But being scared of anything "new" also cripples us as we'd rather be stuck in the same place doing the same thing day-in and day-out.

Something I'll repeatedly say until all of my peers understand it is *potential is not promising*. Embodying your potential and becoming your potential are two different things. When we embody potential to be or do something that means it is in our ability to complete that task. But we first have to make the conscious decision to work towards completing that task in order to become our potential.

Sometimes it takes for us to see someone we know living out their full potential to step up our game – and that's fine! I always say any motivation that puts fire under our butt's is good motivation! We see celebrities making moves and making money constantly, but because we have this conception of celebrities being foreign beings who are "supposed" to live like that, we think nothing of it.

For some of us it's different to see someone we know personally live out their potential and chase their dream! Instead of initially celebrating and admiring that individual's work, we sometimes grow envious and judgmental of that person's decisions. Not long after that we begin to pity ourselves as we compare our current circumstance to someone else's!

Whether it's a public figure or someone you grew up with, someone else shining will only dim your light if you allow it to. Don't let the sight of someone else going after what they want intimidate you – it should instead ignite a fire within you to get your own ball rolling!

Remember that while you're sitting still and thinking about what it is you want to do, someone is out there moving to make it happen! I don't know about you but I want to be in the category of the doers and not the talkers.

We have to learn how to turn intimidation into inspiration! Rather than be jealous of someone for believing in themselves, we should admire that and be honest with ourselves about why we're not in that position. We all envision ourselves as our absolute best and sometimes we might even fantasize about how it would be to live everyday as that person!

I want to note that it is an amazing quality to be able to see yourself in a positive light! That means that no matter what others have said or thought about you, you know you're capable of achieving great things – and that self-confidence should be celebrated! However, having that vision is only the first part to a three-part-plan!

The second part is having a game plan! Once we have the vision of who we want to be, we have to create a strategic plan that will help us become that person. Of course doors can be opened for us, and opportunities might even present themselves, but it's solely up to us to put ourselves in a position to receive everything those opportunities have to offer us.

Do you need to save money to relocate? Should you start working on building a better professional relationship with your professor or advisor? These are examples of minor moves that will make a major difference in positioning you for your next phase!

No matter what field you are in or what dreams you have, networking is fundamental for almost everybody on this journey. Networking is when you interact with people in order to share information and develop contacts, more specifically to further your career. While this can be an intimidating experience, it is one of the most humbling and valuable experiences you'll have on this journey.

Do your homework and see if there are any events you could possibly attend where experts in your field will be! Are there any organizations that will allow you to volunteer or job shadow where you could possibly gain an advisor? It's important to get things like this all figured out so that you can plan to show up and stand out!

The third and final part is enacting that game plan! Putting your plan into motion is the last and most important aspect of becoming your potential. It's typically this stage that freaks us out and we hit the nearest exit as soon as we justify giving up! We've all been there. But now it's time to end that behavior for good!

Time is something we receive and use every day that we're alive, but it's never returned to us to reuse. We can't afford to continue to hold off on our purpose as if we'll be around forever! So the ideas have crossed your mind, you've come up with a plan to execute those ideas, and now you have to do something about it - but how? How do you just one day start living your dream? It's more of a mindset than an action.

What I mean by that is once you make up in your mind you're going to stop at nothing to achieve your goals, you have to carry yourself in a way that exudes that decision. The very day that you consider your future in all of your decisions is the day you start walking in your purpose – you then begin to evolve into the best version of you!

Remaining focused on the bigger picture for our lives and not "living in the moment" so much makes us stronger individuals and it's that very strength that carries us through the journey of fulfilling our purpose.

I think becoming the person we know we can be will be easier to do once we truly believe we deserve that life. We can't treat our aspirations as an impossible task and continue to let other people distract, intimidate, or stop us. There's so much power in taking control of your life and doing what makes you whole; and that kind of empowerment can bring forth nothing but success.

We're so immune to struggling to be satisfied that we don't realize that we can change the course of our life with one decision. The moment you decide to do everything in your power to live the life you dream of is the moment your life changes forever. You'll never think the same way, or live the same way again. From that moment on everything becomes a learning tool to help you maneuver through the process of making your dream a reality.

Deciding to awaken the potential inside of you will bring forth several challenges. One of the first things you may notice is how people start to treat you differently. They will try to bring up who you used to be or what you used to do in a way that accuses you of "changing" as an insult.

The thing these types of people don't understand is that "changing" is required in order to transform into the individual you were created to be! We're not automatically morphed into greatness with no personal effort – we have to evolve and mature in order to successfully fulfill our purpose.

Don't let small-minded people convince you that remaining stagnant is the way to go!

Another challenge you may face when awakening your potential is the feeling of seclusion. When you take a right when everyone is going left it can feel lonely indeed! This is one of the prices you pay for choosing to work towards your dream life when some people around you aren't doing the same.

It's normal to feel like nobody really understands where you are in life because not everyone around you has been equipped or prepared to understand you on that level just yet – especially when they're not evolving within their own lives. This is why it's important to find ways to remind yourself that everything you're enduring will be worth it in the end. You may have to contact an advisor and share your struggles, or call a good friend and vent a little.

We wear one hundred different hats on a daily basis and because life gets hectic *often*, it's important to always make sure we're wearing the right hats at the right times so that we're always on our A-game! However, I want to chat a little about one specific hat. And that hat is **Professionalism***!*

Some of us are naturally spontaneous while others are naturally outgoing; *but no matter what our natural assets are, all of us should work at being professionals.* Carrying yourself a certain way makes all of the difference in how the world sees and responds to you!

Perseverance will get you into the work force, but professionalism will keep you there; which in turn will open doors that will further your career in whatever field you're pursuing. The older we get, the more important professionalism has to become in our daily lives.

As a young adult, feeling attractive is liberating! Making memories and having a blast while doing so is exciting! But **being professional is essential if you ever want to evolve!** _It's important to keep in mind that there is power in professionalism_. However, being professional goes beyond wearing a blazer with a pair of expensive shoes; **being professional is a way of life**.

So what exactly is required of a young professional?

- Hold your vision and trust the process.

- Protect your dream.

- Remember that it's not always what you know, but *who* you know. (network! network! network!)

- Be professional in every aspect of your life (our professionalism shouldn't have an on/off switch).

- Complete every task given to the best of your ability, no matter how minor or major it may be! You never know who's watching you!

- Respect other people's time and don't waste your own.

- Only compete with the person you were yesterday (focus on bettering yourself, not being better than others).

- Keep in mind that every decision develops your destiny.

__Something To Think About__: If you ever question your level of professionalism, I want you to honestly evaluate yourself in this fresh, more modern way:

"If an employer at my dream job were to use my online profile as my resume', would they see anything that would prevent them from hiring me?".

LEADERS FINSIH FIRST

The best way I can describe a leader is someone who makes wise and impactful decisions that guide others into a positive direction as a result! We are given opportunities to make leader-like decisions on a daily basis. Whether or not we take advantage of those opportunities is entirely up to us!

So often we look to someone else to make a choice first in order for us to make up our own minds. Why is that? Why do we deny our ability to affirmatively act on what our heart is telling us to do? I believe a part of this is due to how pop culture has diluted the idea behind *identity*.

Rather than our identity being a quality that distinguishes us from everyone else, it's become a facade that we have to adopt in order to make us similar to everyone else. In today's world, you're not much of an asset *unless you appear to be like the majority*. But it's ironic that being like the majority doesn't leave you with much of an identity at all.

Pop culture can be so invasive that it robs us of the opportunity or space to identify who we really are before it tells us who to be. Especially if you're coming of age in this current generation, it's extremely challenging to grab ahold of your purpose when gaining popularity seems to be the more beneficial move.

Pop culture shows us that people are happier and their lives are better when society "likes" them. Life is better when the masses approves of you, right? Wrong! When you live for the applause of others you will surely die from the rejection of those same individuals. Don't ever put your value into someone else's hands except for your own!

The best part of being a leader is having the courage to make your own path and walk through it whether someone follows you or not!

This chapter isn't titled "Leaders Finish First" for the purpose of rushing this journey in a competitive manner to become successful before the next person who's grinding does. I've said over and over how this journey of pursuing our dream is not a race and it will not happen overnight. But we should become very competitive when it comes to the old version of ourselves versus the new and improved version of ourselves.

We should make it a priority every day to be better than who we were the day before! This becomes a little easier when we look at this competition through a certain lens. The "old" us may have been someone who procrastinated, doubted ourselves, and would rather make an excuse instead of a strategic move. Imagine how long it'd take for someone like that to accomplish even the simplest task let alone pursuing a lifelong dream!

Now, if we look at how the new and improved version of ourselves is proactive, consistent, and disciplined, imagine how much sooner we'd reach our goals and move on to our next phase!

If leadership doesn't seem to come naturally to you, and it doesn't for many of us, don't count yourself out! Sometimes it's scary to speak up when others are used to you being silent. It can be intimidating to have all on eyes on you! Being a leader is a skillset that you have the ability to learn and master if you want to embody it bad enough.

In essence becoming a leader is both easy and beneficial. However, in reality, practicing leadership is very challenging. I say this because being a leader means that you take the high road at all times – no matter the situation. And taking the high road these days is the most unpopular act I can think of right now. It's uncommon to see individuals go against popular opinion; simply due to the fear of being criticized for doing what's right instead of what's popular.

The reason this is so uncommon is because we're not taught about what true strength is. Naturally, we see strength in numbers. The more people there are, the stronger they appear to be. But let's analyze that logic.

If there's an army of one-hundred soldiers standing against one person – does each soldier of that army necessarily need to be strong in order to win? No, simply because there's so many of them that their **combined** efforts will cause some sort of fatality. Now let's discuss the one soldier this army is standing against. In order to stand alone against a full army, there has to be a certain level of confidence, courage, and strength that this one soldier embodies.

While some people might call this one solider an idiot for standing alone against one-hundred other soldiers, most people will recognize his courage before anything and wonder how it must feel to be so confidently isolated. To me, it's more beneficial to take after the brave loner than to be like the weaker soldiers who can only fight because he has backup for when he gets knocked down!

I've always wondered why leadership isn't promoted in pop culture. There's so much talk about money, fame, and fortune that we don't realize how incomplete these fantasies are. Social media revolves around polishing the surface of who we wish to be rather than attend to the substance within us.

Sure, we've heard and seen some moving success stories of some prominent people who seem to have it all figured out. They appear to be the epitome of the diluted definition of success with not a care in the world! We're given the 'what' but are never given the 'how'.

How will we be able to make a list of goals if we don't know ourselves? How will we reach those goals if we don't believe in ourselves? And how in the world can we live out our full potential if we're not strong enough to walk alone during times everyone around us may seem distracted? It's impossible!

There's no way we can effectively go after our aspirations without knowing exactly who we are and why the aspiration is important to us – and that's the part that pop culture refuses to address.

We're required to be "followers" to even participate and engage with the masses through social media! As farfetched as it may seem to many, that's not a coincidence.

The social media world does such a good job of setting up this pyramid that puts famous, popular, and accepted individuals at the top while regular people like you and me hold them up at the bottom. Nevertheless, society is generous enough to give us all ample opportunities to rise to the "top" and be accepted by everyone but only under certain conditions - which isn't generosity at all, rather manipulation.

It's almost like there's a contract we have to sign in order to be "successful". As long as we abide by someone else's rules and compromise our peace of mind for few dollars, we'll be good for life. My aim is to unabashedly speak against this arrangement and advocate for the pure pursuit of internal satisfaction without the consideration of what others may think, say, or feel!

I have countless memories of adults speaking to me as a child and telling me how much of a leader I was and how fortunate I should have felt because not all of my peers possessed the same quality. It never made sense to me that being able to both walk in my truth and positively influence people along the way was a "gift". To me, it was my norm. It wasn't until I grew older, and observed my peers being mentally attacked without them knowing it, that I understood how so many of us could lack leadership.

Unfortunately, there are hundreds of people who can't stand tall without stepping on someone else in the process. And if that type of person sees an ounce of power and purpose inside of you, they will try to destroy it before you see it for yourself; simply because it's impossible to manipulate an awakened individual who knows what they are capable of!

So many of us have been told what our limits are our entire lives and we have grown accustomed to limiting ourselves every day as we hand over our power, influence, and purpose to someone who "appears" to be more deserving of it. It's time-out for that sort of generosity! We can't afford to give away our responsibility to make a difference in the world around us.

We each have been given a purpose that is designed to encourage, enlighten, and empower those around us in our own unique way. Using that voice when others want so badly for you to be silent makes you a leader – and it makes you significant.

The key to leadership is having an unwavering confidence in your ability to make sound decisions that positively affect you as well as those around you! It's your job to set the tone for how others react to you. If you doubt yourself, people will pick up your own habit and doubt everything you do. On the contrary, once you believe in yourself to the point where you confidently make strides toward your goal, those who are watching you will follow and believe in you as well.

You'll notice when you begin to carry yourself as a leader, people will flock to you for guidance and encouragement. They'll feel the force inside of you and will inquire about how to embody it themselves. That's the effect that being a leader will have on others!

It's best to prepare now to "be there" for a lot of people – even when you might not want to be. This may become a challenge when you are dealing with your own issues or doubts and it seems like everyone else wants you to have the answers for their problems!

It's important to remember that having someone look up to you during your time of distress is a positive thing! It may sound strange - but hear me out. When we're going through hard times, everything around us is overshadowed with a darkness that makes it hard to see the bright side of anything. We all go through it at one time or another!

However, having the traits of a leader automatically equips you to be the strong tower for others even at your weakest point. And whether or not we realize this in the moment, It's a blessing. It's an honor to be able to lift someone else up after you've been knocked down yourself. This means that when we feel even a little worthless and defeated someone else thought enough of us to ask for our input and support – which means we're needed, no matter what our circumstance tells us. That kind of strength is admirable and is what we need more of in the world.

As I'm working on concluding this chapter, and book, I'm finding that there is no precise way to "end" it. This subject of identifying our purpose and being focused enough to walk in that purpose is everlasting. There's so many aspects to address and each of them are just as important as the other. So I sit here, struggling to end it. Probably because I know each day societal pressures become more forceful and more of our youth are becoming distracted.

I know that this book only scratches the surface of the issue of purpose versus popularity. And it is my plan to dig deeper into it, and soon. But for now, I want you to use this project of mine as a resource to begin the task of awakening your purpose and go after that grand goal of yours that seems unreachable to many.

You were built to win – but in order to win, you have to start fighting!

A letter from me to you,

There was a time that we as a people took pride in walking in our own purpose and contributing something fresh and valuable to society. I remember when hit television shows glorified two-parent households, promoted honest and transparent friendships, and celebrated college-educated and established minorities! Having a purpose and proudly fulfilling it was popular. Years ago people did acts of kindness because it enriched their lives and not because they could post it for the world to see and receive recognition for it. Once upon a time we strived to be knowledgeable and were willing to fight against both social and political barriers to obtain that knowledge. It's obvious that we have recently fallen away from this mentality. The need of culture reform is not only necessary for us to individually make sound decisions and live fuller lives, but also for the children whose futures are in our hands right at this moment. They deserve to mature in a culture that prioritizes purpose and civil duty – but they can only do so if we revive that way of life.

There's no way around admitting or acknowledging that times have certainly changed. Technology advances daily and resources for connecting with those around the world are widespread. Is this a bad thing?

No. I don't believe that pop culture negatively influencing us is the issue. I believe the issue is our inability and unwillingness to positively influence pop culture.

We act as if we have no power entirely too much. At some point we have to grow tired of allowing others to construct our mind and actions. I'm not saying we should revert back to the early 1900's and not have ability to use social networks! I'm saying we should learn how to properly use social networks and not allow it to use us.

There should be an emphasis put on the understanding of who we are before we boast about what we want or what we have done. It concerns me that our lives are passing us by and most of us are achieving very little of what we aspire to do!

Who are you when the world isn't watching? What would you love to do for the rest of your life – even without receiving a paycheck for it? What is it that gives you that childlike carelessness and freedom? If you know the answers to these questions – turn the phone off for a while, disconnect your internet and try to spend more time **doing** these things away from the pressures or expectations of others.

If you don't know the answers to the questions I asked, try to spend more time **finding** the answers away from the pressures and expectations of others! Discovering this personal information and incorporating it into our everyday lives will add a value that will ensure we are each indeed successful.

-E